Monumenta Indica Series No.–6

Philosophy of Bhagavan Sri Ramana Maharishi

Nagesh D. Sonde

Sri Satguru Publications
A Division of
Indian Books Centre
Delhi - India

Published by
Sri Satguru Pubiications,
Indological and Oriental Publishers
A Division of
Indian Books Centre
40/5, Shakti Nagar,
Delhi-110007
India

Email: ibcindia@vsnl.com
Website: http://www.indianbookscentre.com

First Edition: Delhi, 1995
Reprinted . Delhi. 2005

ISBN 81-7030-472-5

Printed at Chawla Offset Printers, Delhi 110 052

Philosophy of Bhagavan Sri Ramana Maharishi

Contents

Introduction

In taking up the study of the Teachings of Bhagavan Sri Ramana Maharishi, I have attempted to take assistance of his recorded words, giving explanatory notes wherever required. I have, however, found it not necessary to quote the extracts from the Talks, as they are recorded, because they were not written by Bhagavan himself, and there could be divergence between the words spoken by him and what was recorded by the devotees. Yet there is no doubt that care was taken to make the message as authentic as possible, especially referring them to Bhagavan wherever was found necessary.

Even then while the Tamil, Telugu or Malayalam versions may said to be fully authentic, assuming that Bhagavan had gone through all the manuscripts himself, the same cannot be said about the translations available in English language. This is because many of the Sanskrit words cannot be really translated in English language without often distorting the meaning entirely. Besides the English language used in the translations also often appears too colloquial and archaic. Therefore, the sentences had to be redrafted to convey the central message, consistent with explanations given by Bhagavan on different occasions. The importance of these Talks, however, cannot be and has not been minimized.

It would be presumptuous on my part or to that matter on the part of any one to claim that he has fully imbibed the

Teachings of Bhagavan or to that matter of any teacher. In fact no one ever claims to be so. If any one has really imbibed the teachings, then that person will not waste his time in talking, let alone attempt writing a book about them. He will remain in silent adoration of the Bliss of knowing the Self.

Therefore, no scholarship nor any spiritual realisation need be attached to this attempt towards this study. It is confirmed view of the present writer that Teachers are not meant to pass on their own views as a precept, faith or a dogma to be followed by the persons who come after them. Their essential role, as they have repeatedly emphasised, is to make the aspirants receptive to perceive the Truth, as it really is, by putting them on the Path, the Way, which would lead them to Truth and all the while guiding, supporting and encouraging them, as the occasion would demand, while the aspirant himself walks on the Path.

Sri Shankara has clearly mentioned that even the Vedas cannot deliver one from the Samsara; they can only guide the aspirants in their search for deliverance. "*jnapakam hi shastram na tu karakam iti stithih*". And again, "*Sahstradidameva bhavati, idam ishta sadhanam, idam anishtasadhanam iti sadhyasadhana sambandha vishesha abhivyaktih*"

The Path had to be traversed by the aspirant himself and no one, not even the Teacher can traverse it for him. Any attempt or claim by any one, howsoever great a Teacher he might be, that he can deliver the aspirant without the aspirant having to do anything, is travesty of truth. Such person should be shunned for they are, verily, the impediments on the Way, the Path.

There is a statement attributed in Zen Buddhism, which is relevant here. The means, the symbols, the idols, the gods and even the Bodhisatva are only an assistance or aids like the staff which traveller carries on his travels. They are to be carried and made use of only so long their need is felt in traversing the Path. Once the person is confident of walking on his own legs then these aids are required to be dispensed with.

Even the Upanishadic Teachers subscribed to this Truth. In Maitri Upanishad (IV.5-6), it is clarified thus. " 'Fire, Air, Sun, Time, whatever it is, Breath, Food, Brahma, Rudra, Vishnu, some meditate upon one, some upon another. Tell us which one is best for us'. Then he said to them, 'These are but the chief forms of the Supreme, the immortal, the bodiless Brahman. To whichever one each man is devoted here, in his world he rejoices. For it has been said, 'Verily, this whole world is Brahman. Verily, these which are its chief forms one meditate upon, worships and discards. For with these one moves higher and higher in the worlds. And when all things perish, he attains unity with the Person, yes, with the Person' ".

The present writer is fully aware of this fact. Therefore, his very attempt to write this book shows that he is still on the Path and he needs all the aids, all the thoughts recorded in the Talks and all the words contained in many other books as well. His attempt in this book is but his groping step on the path which he obviously is treading. Therefore the contents of the following pages are to be understood only as comprehension by his intellect and not the product of the clarity of his experience nor the illumination of the Truth spoken by Bhagavan.

An attempt has been made to serially and logically present the basic principles of Bhagavan Sri Ramana Maharishi's Teachings, so that they may be able to grasped by one who is reasonable given to intellectual introspection.

This may enable one, as it did to the author to realise in course of time the way to the place of abidance, which is the heart, with the Self present therein, the Bliss of Being, which is the purpose and the goal on that journey. Then perhaps, it would be possible to dispense the aids one by one, which he had taken assistance of.

I

In the spiritual tradition of India, it is accepted as cardinal principle that whenever the Perennial Principles (*Dharma*) get obscure and there is rise in unrighteousness the Supreme Lord energies Himself and manifests so that *Dharma*, (the Perennial Principles), *Rta* (the Cosmic Law) and Satya (the Truth) can again be established. But the belief, however, that the Supreme Lord comes down Himself, in all His Entirety, in human form to participate in the normal life and thereby guide the affairs of the world, belongs undoubtedly to the realm of poetic fancy.

One who is given to rational attitude and influenced by the intellect and sense of discrimination would rarely accept such generalisations, which are not the product of reflection or the result of meditative experience. Therefore, they neither convince the intellect nor create an experience in the heart. Therefore the true Teacher does not expect the aspirant to be a blind follower of a tradition, a faith, a belief, dogma or a religion or even to his own words communicated to assist him on his spiritual journey. He expects the aspirant to be receptive to his logical thought and his intuitive experiences.

If it is accepted as a reasonable premise that Creation is at the instance of a power or an energy, whether that power be called Brahman, the Supreme Lord or by any other name and further that He has pervaded whatever that has been created, then it reasonable to accept that He must have also manifested in each of his creations, though this fact may not be evident or realised in the normal circumstances by each of his creation.

If the above premise is accepted then, each human being, must have within himself the spark of divinity and the capacity to realise the identity with the manifestation of the Supreme Being in his own Self and by his own Self. And of all the creatures, the human being, being the most perceptive, having keen sense of intelligence and perception and capable of power of discrimination, he should be able to realise and experience this divine essence.

There is, in fact, the possibility of being receptive of the inner Divinity, which has already manifested in each human being with signs visible. This, however, depends on the extent to which each person has the capacity of Perception (Darshana) and at what point of time he is presently standing. Only when such is the position, only then would there be possibility of consummation of this inner energy, becoming externally visible in physical, mental and intellectual spheres.

The Bhagavad Gita calls such consummation, 'mad bhaava aagatah' - being in communion with Me. It is like being born afresh energised by the illumined Light of the Supreme Godhead. The extent and depth to which these two, the inner spiritual illumination and its outward intellectual and physical expression act, inter-act and influence one another depends on the stage at which the aspirant has reached. The true Teacher who can perceive this subtle state of being does give a knowing 'push' to the efforts of the aspirant so that he may reach towards the consummation and communion with the Supreme Being, the Brahman.

In the case of Bhagavan Sri Ramana Maharishi, this consummation and communion took place not as a result of any sadhana or intense personal effort but suddenly as a flash of lightning. As graphically put in Kathopanishad (IV.4), "Of this Brahman, there is this teaching; this is, as it were, like the lightening which flashes or the winking of the eye." In his case the ground preparation, probably, must have been through eons of ages ere this consummation took place. None can foresee the moment when this moment arrives, and till it arrives, each person reacts like any other person.

While the concept of descent of the Supreme Energy in the fullness of its glory is assured only in times of decline unrighteousness and the consequent need to re-establish righteousness, the consummation and communion of an individual person and the Divine Spark can take place any time during his lifetime. This gives a meaning and substance to his life and aspirations. Valmiki of the ancient age or a Tulsidas of the modern age a person can expect to have such consummation any time, even when he is not consciously aware and ready.

When such event takes place the person will experience himself slow and subtle transformation first internally and later externally, as the consequential effect of the internal consummation, the potentiality being transformed as the possibility, making his external life reflect the internal power or energy, or the Spark so that he could continue to be an active participant and instrument of the Divine Intent, Play or the 'Lila'. He becomes the nimitta, the apparent instrument of the Supreme Consciousness, of the Supreme Bliss, having dual dimension, externally the human Spirit reflecting the Divine Spark within.

Bhagavan exhibited this facet of Divinity very much in his early life, in an extremely subtle manner where the Divine Spark takes control over the Gross human frame, where the Divine Consciousness, Divine Power and Divine Intent manifests inspite of the outward limitations and infirmities of the human body, making each moment, each event and each circumstance vibrant with spiritual ardour.

In such satiation, the individual's role ceases to be different or independent of the Power within, but becomes the arche type of the Divine Essence to lead, guide, point out, encourage the aspirants through actions which are palpably human. Therefore, it would be great error to see Bhagavan having taken the birth for any other reason other than as the instrument of the Divine Consciousness.

There is an important declaration made by Sri Krishna in Bhagavad Gita (IX.27) "Whatever actions you perform, whatever you eat, whatever you offer, whatever you give, whatever austerities you practice - do those , O Son of Kunti, as ordained by Me" and further in (XI.33), he says. "By Me alone are they (the Kaurava heroes) slain already. You be merely the apparent cause, O Arjuna". As a consequence of which the duality between the actions of the Devotee and of the Divinity becomes destroyed. And "*atma tvam, girija matih, sahacharah pranah, shareeram griham, pooja me vishayopabhogacharana, nidra samadhistitih, sancharah padayoh, pradakshinavidhih stotrani sarvagiro, yadyat karma karomi tat tad akhilam Shambho tavaradhanam*" .

The crisis in which the Lord appears, therefore, need not necessarily be the crisis of immense magnitude in empirical sense in the life of human beings, it could also be in a crisis which is intensely personal to each human being. For the person who is aware of the void within his Self and becomes receptive to the Divine Spark or the resonance of the Divine Sound, there could be a possibility of consummation and communion with the Divine descent and the ascent of the human spirit. The significance of such an event would be evident in each case and in each action of such human being when his influence pervades, when his actions speak louder even when he seems to be not acting at all, or when his speech is heard even when he is silent, or when his movement is sensed even when he is at rest. His way and the field of his action would not visible to the ordinary human eye nor discernible to the superficial mind but is perceived only when the Mind and Consciousness carefully receptive and perceptive.

Bhagavan insisted that spiritual aspiration and effort is always an individual endeavour. Each one on his own should enquire within, because the doubts, the problems, the miseries, the all enemies all emanate from within one's own Self. Therefore, the field of the battle is also within. While the Lord will always will remain to be the Charioteer, and his grace, his assistance would continue to steer the wayward horses of the aspirants he would never commit himself to assure Realisation of Truth as a matter of his personal dispensation.

Sri Ramana was reluctant to accept disciples in the traditional manner or initiate the aspirants through some secret *Mantra* or recommend any particular *Sadhana* or even venture to lay down rules and regulations for normal life, or define the role or the works which are temporal and conventional in nature. His entire sphere of activity was concentrated on the psychological and supra-conscious level of each individual person, which was quite different from the one enjoined by other Teachers. While outer spiritual practices were not discouraged his emphasis was always on amplification of the internal consciousness, which is beyond the pale of human thought, social or conventual social practices. The signs, the symbols, the suggestions were all to be used within, to be understood and practiced by one who is receptive, *shraddhaavaan*, so that the Light of the Self can illumine the passage to Eternal Bliss.

Therefore, Bhagavan's philosophy is not to be 'learnt' from the recorded talks or the words of explanations given, because there is nothing to be learned from his words for he has said nothing new, what others have not said earlier. The

Vedas have recorded it, the Upanishads have reflected and meditated upon it, the Commentators have discussed on it. Yet there is much to be received from Bhagvan Sri Ramana Maharishi, the way he lived his life, the way he enquired about the eternal question "Who am I" and the manner of his benign guidance which he bestowed on the aspirants.

Sri Ramana Maharishi was not a teacher or preacher in the conventional sense. He was like Sri Dakshinamurti, the World Teacher, who would communicate the Truth in silent gestures and pithy replies, which appeared often to be repetitive. But then Truth is ever repetitive, because it does not change with time or with clime. Enquire within yourself the question 'Who am I'? Possibly, the word 'replies' may not be the appropriate word to be used. Because, in the endeavour, in this adventure recommended by Bhagavan there is no scope for replies to be given, no solutions to be offered. Every effort is an individual adventure; therefore every clarification or realisation is also an individual experience.

In the luminous Light everything becomes clear without having to be clarified, everything becomes understood without having to be explained, everyone becomes wise without being instructed and every one becomes Aware without having to be told about being aware. As Sri Shankara remarks in Viveka Chudamani, "How could that Brahman who Himself is like the sky without impurity, beyond imagination, without limits, without motions, without modifications, void within and without, unlike any other thing, second to none, be the subject matter for knowledge ?" The Truth is '*svatah-siddha*' - self-valid certainty, '*svayam-siddha*' - self-existent, '*svayam-sakshi*' - self-certifying.

The human being is conditioned by the views, opinions, values, moral and ethical standards of his generation as well as by those compendium of thoughts which have come to be handed over by the past generations. The moment he is born his mind shapes his character and his actions direct his future purpose in life. The entirety of his mind inextricably weaves the pattern of his life, web of human values, the samsara.

In normal behaviour his mind directs his attention outside himself. Therefore he perceives multiplicity of experiences. When he turns his attention inward and gives himself to introspection, then he finds his field not constrained by empirical thought-responses. Not bound by the senses and the thoughts, he lives in the breath of freedom, where no thought provokes his mind, no concept captivates his imagination, no rule regulates his behaviour nor any purpose hinders his action. He has all the freedom of his Self, the bliss of his Self, to be creative in the extra-ordinary power of the Mind, the natural vibrancy of which was hitherto was hidden behind the layers of the thoughts.

It is to this field, to this power of the Mind, to this world of spirit to which Bhagavan desires to guide and lead the aspirant, so that through his own enquiry, through his own experience, through his own perception, the aspirant may be lead, like the father to the son, like the teacher to the disciple, to reach the Revelation, the Realisation and the Revalidation of the Blissful Truth within, which he essentially is but of which he is temporarily un-aware of. On that path, as said earlier, the aspirant may need in the beginning crutches of the intellect, the scriptures, the reason and rationality with full knowledge that a time may come, will surely come when these crutches will certainly have to be to cast on the wayside, so that we may walk rest of the Path with clarity of vision and contentment in the heart.

II

Among the many who came in close contact with Bhagavan Sri Ramana Maharishi, Sri Vashishtha Ganapati Muni was the most erudite. He had both intellectual brilliance and spiritual awareness to be receptive to the Light emanating from Bhagavan. A great Sanskrit scholar and adept in the Vedas, Upanishads and the auxiliary texts, he had also the competence over speech to make Bhagavan's intention known to the world at large. Earlier it was Shri Sivaprakash Pillai, Shri Gambhiram Sheshayya, Shri Natesh Mudaliar and later Sri Ganapati Muni who elicited great number of clarifications regarding the nature of Truth from Bhagavan himself. There were others like F. H. Humphreys, Paul Brunton, C.C Cohen, Arthus Osborne who made the personality of Bhagavan known far and wide.

However, while others appear to have received the teachings far and in between, Ganapati Muni, who was known as Nayana, and Kavyakantha, was among the first ones who had the intense austerity to grasp the significance and the relevance of the clarifications given by Bhagavan. He was a '*rishi, jnanatriptah, kritatmanah, vita raga prasantah*' – a seer, satisfied in wisdom, perfect in Self, free from passion and tranquil.

It is reported that Nayana, inspite of being a great scholar of Sanskrit language and a highly spiritual aspirant, was wandering all over India in search of illumination, which was alluding him inspite of his vast erudition in Vedic lore and *Mantra Shastra.* All his efforts had borne no fruits and he was travelling from place to place in search of such one person who would lead him from Darkness to Light.

On one such travels he had come over to south to Tiruvannamalai, the seat of Lord Arunachala. Some of the people who were dazzled by the brilliance of the wisdom of this mendicant and seeing him yet not having peace of mind nor contentment in heart, suggested that he should visit the Brahmin Swami who was then dwelling on the Arunachala hill. He, they said, was one who was seeped in penance and shining in illumination like Lord Shiva himself.

Nayana himself has described his first encounter with the Brahmin Swamy. "It was the 9th day of Kartik festival (Monday, the 18th November 1907) when I fell at the feet of the Maharishi, with both my hands clasping his feet, the right hand grasping the right foot and the other, with the left." The scholar of Shastras that he was, he considered it inauspicious to touch the right foot of the Master with the left hand.

He implored Bhagavan, like Narada to Sanatkumara, that he had mastered all the Vedas, the Upanishads, the rituals and the Mantra Shastra but he had neither peace nor any illumination inspite of all his *Tapas*. Is he on the right path? The Brahmin Swami, who till then had not been speaking to any body, opened his gracious lips for the first time, and said: "If one watches whence the notion 'I' arises, then the mind is absorbed in That; That is *Tapas*. When a *Mantra* is repeated, if one watches the Source from which the resonance of the *Mantra* is produced, the mind is absorbed in That. That is *Tapas*."

Sri Ganapati Muni stood transfixed with wonder. A great knower of scriptures that he was, he had for the first time been told by one to shift his attention from thoughts to the Thinker, from knowledge to the Knower. This transformed the entire spectrum of his thought and vision, as when the entire world gets illumined all at once when the lightning strikes. He gazed at the calm and serene face of the Brahmin Swami, and experienced therein the depth of eternity, even as abundant Grace from the Swami was flowing on him continuously and uninterruptedly. He realised that this was not an ordinary person but a great Seer, a veritable Bhagavan himself. He called him thereafter Maharishi, a great Seer. Later, when he came to know the name of the Swami to be Venkataraman, he shortened it to Ramana, Bhagavan Sri Ramana Maharishi.

This is a great event in understanding the teachings of Sri Ramana, since these first words continued to be his refrain to prod the aspirants to inquire themselves for the answers, even as he was supplying some clues here and some clarifications there. And if one really desires to understand what Bhagavan had to convey, then one has to keep some moments free from the captivating compassion and irredeemable influence which one is like to have in his presence.

There have been many books on the life of Bhagavan, and it is not intention of the present writer to repeat the events of his temporal life. How as a child, he appeared to be ordinary and inconspicuous among his brothers and friends; how he got the experience of death and how he left his uncles's residence to go to his permanent abode, at the feet of Lord Arunachala – all these and many more events have been recorded by the devotees in his presence and some of which, we are informed, were approved by Bhagavan himself.

Bhagavan wrote very little himself except some songs in adoration to Lord Arunachala. 'Who am I ?' 'The Forty Verses', '*Ulladu Narpadu*' (Sat-Darshanam) or '*Unnadhi Nalubadhi*' (Upadesha Saram) were not written as composite documents but were stray replies on pieces of paper or verses composed on different occasions. These were collected later by his devotees in a book form. These appeared first in Tamil language and were later translated in Sanskrit and other regional languages, including English.

A statement which he made to Shri Devaraja Mudaliar makes his views clear about writing books. He obviously realised the limitations which the spoken word places on the pure experience. All words are projections of the mind, he said. The more you exercise the mind and more success you have in composing the verses the less peace you have. What use is it to acquire such accomplishments if you don't acquire peace ? There is possibility, therefore, that there could be imperceptible difference between the statements made by Bhagavan and as they came to be recorded or as translated. But it should nevertheless be conceded that the talks record with devotion and faith, contained the essence of his thoughts, as can be seen from the manner he lived his life.

One wonders, therefore, whether one could make out any distinct philosophy of his own, which gives distinctive mark to his expressions, or he was happy to explain the basic principles of Truth, the Bliss which he was experiencing. He was more keen to explain the method which he had used for his 'sadhana' and found useful than the various systems of philosophies (Darshanas), except to clarify what he himself had experienced.

In another statement which Devaraj Mudaliar records, Maharishi clarifies this statement. He said that it never occurred to me to write a book or compose verses. All the poems composed by him were on the request of some one or the other in connection with some event. Even Forty Verses on Reality was not planned as a book but consists of verses composed on different occasions and later arranged in book form by Murugannar and others.

The only poems that came to him spontaneously and compelled him, as it were, to write them, without any one urging him, were the Eleven Stanzas to Sri Arunachala and the Eight Stanzas to Sri Arunachala. The opening words came to him one morning and even though he tried to suppress them saying, 'What I have to do with these words ?' they would not be suppressed till he composed them.

His philosophy, therefore, was his life, the way he lived and the way he guided each aspirant towards their individual salvation. His philosophy was his perception of Truth. It would, therefore, be unproductive to hang on his recorded words, and forget the essence of his message.

What distinguishes Bhagavan from others, however, was the internal consummation of his Individual Self with the Universal Self, which came about as if unaided by any Guru or Teacher. His explanation how such consummation came about, was only for the purpose of guiding the aspirants that they too can have identical experience of Reality if they too enquired about the source of 'I'. His abiding experience in the Bliss of Brahman seemed so secure that even when he explained some of the devotees the contents of the scriptures, there appeared no contradiction.

Our endeavour, therefore, should be more on the manner of his approach to the Truth than his description of the nature of Truth. He also appeared often reluctant to waste time in describing Truth or engaging himself in fruitless polemics. He was more interested on Truth which the aspirants have to realise than the path to be adopted and traversed by them. Therefore, he repeatedly recommended people to dive deep within themselves to realise and revel in the Bliss, which, he assured, we essentially are, rather than devote much of their time on polemics or philosophical discussions. He would as well remind them it would be preferable to taste the Honey than find out the chemical composition of Honey.

It is not proper to compare two great souls. But it must nonetheless relevant to point out that whereas many great sons of India who have revolutionised religious movements in the post Vedic and Upanishadic age, have been to a large extent the commentators of the Eternal Truth which the Vedic Seers had 'Seen'. Sri Ramana came not so much as a commentator, but as a Seer similar to the seers of the Vedas and Upanishads. He spoke from his own experience rather than from the intellectual appreciation and subsequent realisation of the Truth spoken by the ancient seers. If he used to quote the earlier texts it was more as to authenticate his own experience with those who were similarly placed.

Besides, unlike the commentators he had found no necessity to have a Guru for his initiation, outside himself and, therefore, had his own Self as his Guru. He was one like the seers of the Vedas, who 'saw' the Truth unaided other than their own pure Self. Like them he too was 'sakshat krit dharmanah'.

In fact the concept of Guru for Sri Ramana was completely different from the traditional view. He did not deny the traditional belief regarding the necessity of having a Guru. In fact, in reply to a direct question whether a Guru is necessary for spiritual unfoldment, he did not hesitate to mention that there is a Guru for every one. However, the Guru need not necessarily come in human form. He may be an animal, a bird, a python, Earth, the Space, in fact any thing which the Lord in his boundless compassion may make his instrument for Grace.

In the Ultimate analysis, it is the Lord alone who is the Guru, He is said to preside over as the Guru, dwelling in the heart of the human being who seeks to impart the knowledge of Brahman. All others too are but the instruments, nimitta. Sri Dattatreya had twenty four Gurus. Other may have had less number. When Satyakama approaches his teacher with luminous face, he tells that his face shines like one knowing Brahman because he has a Guru who were other than men. The Guru may be internal or external. Sri Ramana admitted a Guru for himself also. For him, however, the Guru was his own SELF.

Speaking about Sadhana also, he had his own distinctive stamp of authority and personal perspective. In fact, he clarified that he was not aware of the meaning of 'Sadhana' till much later time. His sadhana was as natural to him as breathing was. It did not assume any particular discipline in conventional form. Once in reminiscent mood he even remarked that he has never done any sadhana. When he was performing sadhana he did not even know what sadhana was. Only much later he came to know what sadhana was and how many different methods were there. According to him, only if there was any object or anything different from him then he could think of some sadhana for acquiring it. Only if there was any goal to attain, he would have made some sadhana to reach that goal. But there was nothing that he wanted to attain nor any goal that was to be achieved. Therefore, he did not do any special by way of sadhana.

In lighter vein he would remark that he is presently sitting with his eyes open; earlier he was sitting with his eyes closed. That was all the difference. He was not doing any particular sadhana earlier. People said that he was in samadhi because he was sitting with his eyes closed. Since he was not talking, they assumed that he was in mauna, silent meditation. For him nothing could be stranger than this. According to him Self is not attained by doing something or the other, but by doing nothing at all and remaining quiet and allowing one's blissful nature revel in its own glory, unsullied by the external sense-contacts.

In fact, the very first time when he communicated his thoughts to the world by writing on stray pieces of paper, he made his views very clear and unambiguous. He clarified that realisation dawns entirely through constant enquiry of the eternal question "WHO AM I?" or what is the source of 'I', as one normally understand by that word. It does need any external effort but depends entirely on internal perseverance. His approach to Truth was direct and incisive, which has to be austere with intense commitment.

He would reminicised that at an early impressionable age, he was overpowered with the fear of death, even though there was no ostensible reason for such fear. At that time he recollects saying to himself: Well then, this body is dead. It will be carried stiff to the burial ground and there it would be burnt and reduced to ashes. But with the death of this body, am 'I' dead? This body is silent and inert. But I feel the full force of my personality and also the resonance of the sound 'I' within myself distinct from the body. I am, therefore, the DEATHLESS SPIRIT, untouched by death.

It is interesting to see that such realisation came to this remarkable young boy, not through study of any religious scriptures, nor through initiation by any Guru, nor through any ostensible sadhana. It came with sudden illumination or realisation as dawned on the Seers of old, who became aware of the Truth, all of a sudden and in all vivid diversity. Even the Path to Perfection is narrow and steep, with many sign-posts to guide and clarify, to be reached step by step, the awareness itself is immediate and instantaneous. Rarely does realisation seep through the Mind piece by piece or drop by drop. It comes with enormous force as the waters come when the flood gates of the huge dam, are opened. It comes and comes inundating all that comes on it way. It is for this reason that Nayana declared that he was a Maharishi, a great Seer, Bhagavan, the resplendent Lord himself.

Once the sun shines in the sky, he cannot be hidden under a bushel. As days passed into weeks, weeks into months, and months into years, this awareness became more and more stabilised in the whole personality of the young boy and soon the entire world became part of him. He saw himself in everything on which his sight fell, and saw everything in his own Self. He and the Universe of which he was but an infinitely small part were not different. He became one with the stream and sailed as one with the stream. He was neither aware of the day nor of the night, of himself nor of the others. A strange ONE-NESS with the world seems to have overpowered him and the thin line between himself and others vanished and HE WAS, as it were, the ONE he came to see.

As people came to know about Maharishi, they flocked for *Darshana* and benevolence. But he did not seem to be inclined to be the dispenser of munificence but a guide, a Teacher who was intent to show the Path, the Way for deliverance. For every one he had one suggestion: Enquire within your selves for your Self. Find out yourself, who is this 'I', which makes one burdened with sorrow and unhappiness or even enquire who is this 'I' that is asking the question. For every one who approached him for advise and clarification, he would persevere in buttonholing like Socrates and ask them whether they have enquired themselves about their own 'I'?

Enquiry does not mean vulgar curiosity or inane inquisitiveness. It is not even asking the question "Who am I" mechanically and monotonously, without being aware of the question or the process of inquiry. It is the sincere effort to find out the source, which, if found, will inundate and illumine the seeker with revelations.

Therefore one should enquire the source of 'I' or in other words, 'Who am I' ? That would, then, be the real process of 'learning' 'knowing' 'realising' the wisdom of the Seers.

In passing, one may mention that when Bhagavan Sri Ramana left his house he was searching for his 'home'. He found it when he came to the sanctum sanctorum of the great temple of Sri Arunachala at Tiruvannamalai. When he reached the town it is reported that he went straight to the temple and reaching straight the Lord, he announced, " Father I have come". And, indeed, he had reached his 'home' the source of his 'I'. And having come to the source, he had no reason to go anywhere not even to the temple because the temple of the Lord was his Hṛidaya, the heart where his source was found. He was to explain much later the significance of *Hridayam* saying that it means Hrit+Ayama - the source here. Therefore, there was no need for him to go any where. Therefore, in that place he continued to abide. It is rightly said by the teachers of Upanishads, "*atha yad idam asmin brahma-pure daharam pundareekam vesma, daharo'sminn antarikshah, tasmin yad antah, tad anveshtavyam, tad vaa va vijijnasitavyam*" Chandogya Up.VIII.1.1).

III

A reasonable question can be asked. Why should one enquire about 'I', if Grace can be had easily from the Guru and with his power the aspirants can cross the frontiers of this Primordial World ? In what manner would this adventure in the world of Enquiry help us in our day to day battle for peace and contentment, and even for our very survival ? When the stomach is empty and misery is abundant all around, with no hope to be seen on the horizon, of what need would enquiry of things be, of which we are not even aware ? When we cannot solve even the trivial problems of immediate consequence, experienced and suffered each and every day, how can we ever hope to touch even the fringe of the things which are mysterious ?

Sri Shankaracharya has said that this life, *Samsara* is a strange mixture of the Truth and Untruth. In such world of confusion would it not be better if we could be blessed with Grace and thereby be released from the temporal torments ? What is Truth and what is untruth, why all these queries, why all these uncertainties if approach can be made easy and salvation, made palatable ?

But, unfortunately, the Path to Deliverance or for Salvation is neither paved with good intentions nor by easy avenues. They are only paved with sincere austerity and intense perseverance. "Sharp as the edge of a razor and hard to cross, difficult to tread is that path (so) the sages declare", thus was Nachiketa cautioned by Yama in Katha Upanishad.

What is Truth and what is untruth, what is Proper and what is Pleasant – the knowledge of these should, therefore, be the first steps in our enquiry. The Truth of which the wise one speaks is not merely the truth of speech, or of action, or of sight, or of hearing or of thinking; it is all comprehensive and all pervasive. The Proper (Shreya) which the men of wisdom speak is not what is socially proper, or economically justifiable but also what is ethically, morally and spiritually proper as well.

If there is proper understanding of these basics, then we would be in a better position to perceive, discriminate and understand and be aware of the reality of things we observe, what we observe, how we observe, why we observe and who is it that really observes. In other words, our attempts towards enquiry in the Self would be about the Right Path and the Right Perspective. We should be in search of the 'I' with all its ramifications. The Truth essentially is That One by being aware of which we becomes aware of the truth of speech, of action, of seeing, of hearing, of thinking. The Reality then becomes the experience of the Totality and not of the parts and parcels, not a little in the beginning and little more in times to come. All at once, here and now, as "when it is known through every state of cognition, it is rightly known for (by such knowledge) one attains life eternal. Through one's own Self one gains power and through wisdom one gains immortality" (Kena Up.II.4). That which, "Not by speech, not by mind, not by sight, can he be apprehended. How can He be comprehended except by him who says that It Is' " (Katha Up. II.3.12).

It is, therefore, rational and reasonable to assume that when one gets human life and also the accompanying discriminative power, if one does not address oneself to this most important question, the mystery of his life, "WHAT IS TRUTH ?" then the very purpose of his human life seems to be defeated.

Sri Shankara enjoins every seeker of Truth to enquire about the three fundamental questions. "What is it that is called bondage ? How does it come about ? How does it get established ? How could one be liberated therefrom ? What is this that is non-Self ? What is it that is Supreme Self ? How does one discriminate ? Speak to me of these things".

Sri Ramana had his own distinctive manner of looking on these matters of life. He would point out that apart from the statements in Veda, one realises on one's own that wherever there is body, there is also misery. This is the direct experience of each and every person. Therefore, one should enquire into one's true nature which is not dependent on the body.

In another context he remarked that if a man thinks that his happiness is due to external causes and his possessions, then it would also be reasonable to conclude that his happiness would increase with the increase of his possessions and diminish in proportion to their diminution. And if he is without any possessions, then his life should also be without any happiness. The day to day experience, however, neither corroborate such reasoning nor justify such conclusion.

We find many persons having enormous control over riches and possessions and also power and prestige in society. Inspite of these they have sleepless nights, pain and dissatisfaction in their daily life; while others who have no wealth to call their own, are content with the life they lead. This dichotomy is hard to explain, except conclude that happiness does not necessarily depend on possession of wealth and power but it is fundamental and the state of one's mind.

By giving instances, he clarifies that in deep sleep (*sushupti*) the man is without any of his possessions, including his own body. In such circumstances, instead of being unhappy the person seems to be more happy. Every one desires to have sound sleep, and sleep is the state of mind when the modifications, which normally disturb the balance, are at rest, the man experiences the supreme happiness. Therefore, one is constrained to conclude that happiness is the internal state of mind, which being natural to a human being, is not dependent upon external causes. Therefore one must endeavour to seek happiness in mind, which is an internal approach and not possessions of materials and possession which are external in nature. This can be done only by diverting our mind from projecting externally and concentrating it internally. That would make him perceive his own Self, which the Primal Source of all happiness, contentment and bliss.

He further replies that experiences such as 'I went, I came, I was, I did' come to human beings in their natural course. But invariably from these experiences, one is erroneously inclined to assume that the subject matter of all these actions and experiences is the consciousness 'I'. This, however, is a misconception. The actions such as 'going' 'coming' 'doing' are in relation to the gross human body and not to the subtle consciousness 'I' or the Self within.

Similarly, when one says I, my family, my possessions, my house, my city, my nation - all these concepts and assumptions are in relations to the gross body and the thoughts which arise in mind are also in relation to the gross objects. They have nothing to do with the Self which is within. Once there is a severance of the gross things of the body from the subtle Self or the 'I' within, then the Self becomes free, unattached, unfettered and uncontaminated. Even thereafter whenever the 'I' is refereed to, it is in relation to the subtle Self and not the gross body.

The subtle Self goes through many gross bodies, each with their own peculiar and distinct thoughts and memories, to which the Self is not attached with any of these empirical 'I', which is otherwise referred to as Ego. The ego is concerned with the gross body whereas the 'I', the real 'I' or the Self is independent of the gross body. If this fact is understood and realised then no one will associate the state of happiness or unhappiness with the happiness and unhappiness of this gross body.

When people approached Bhagavan for clarifications he would point out this error which lies in human mind in the wrong identification of the Self or the 'I' with the body. Once he said, by way of clarification, that if people feel that Bhagavan is the body then they should refer the queries to his body and not to himself, because he 'knows' that he and his body are quite different. Whereas the body reacts to the stimuli of the senses the Self is independent to the influences of the senses.

But the body does not by itself reply or react to the queries. Therefore one should understand the true nature of the person whom one addresses as Bhagavan. Is he the body ? Assuredly Not. If he is not the body then what is he that is refereed to as Bhagavan ? He is the Self abiding in the body. This understanding is the very first step on the path of being aware of one's Self. Similarly in common parlance when we say 'I', we refer the gross body with all the thoughts and memories, whereas the 'I' is the Self which is not affected by thoughts and the memories, but which used the thoughts and memories in empirical existence. The Self on its own is peaceful and blissful.

How, then, does this misconceptions arise in man ? To such a question he clarifies as follows. It is the Mind which relates the body with the Self. Mind, with all the thoughts, concepts, desires, hopes etc. creates the false ego, a false phenomenon, in which the Mind in turn moves. The false ego gives a shape to the thoughts, concepts, desires hopes etc. and is known as '*ahamkara*' i.e. *Aham-akara* - the I-form. This *ahamkara* or ego along with all the thoughts associates itself with objects; while the Self is the primary subject. Whereas such relationship gives rise to false sense of 'I', a serene sense of disinterest with temporal objects gives the real 'I', the Self the substance to Reality.

Therefore, one should not confuse oneself with the thoughts, concepts, things which are created by the modifications of the mind, giving form and separate identity to the false ego. One's movements within the sphere of this false ego causes misery. When one is said to be miserable inspite of wealth and possessions, it is the possessions of these notions which makes one think of himself to be this, that or the other; or to possess this, that or the other.

There is fable in Buddhist religion. Buddha told one of the kings that one become miserable with the things which we seek most, love most, desire to possess most. When the king did not understand this, he was enquired by the great Buddha: would you not be more miserable losing your wife, your children, your kingdom, your people ? When the king agreed it to be so, then Buddha told him to reflect on these things. Then the king came to realise that wealth, possession, relationships have substance in connection with the body and not with the Self. Thus the king became a follower of the precepts of the Buddha.

If we consider our relationship with our ancestors, or the relationship of ourselves with 'our own near and dear ones' then we would realise on reflection that our relationship with our ancestors and descendants has some thing to do with our gross body and not with our Self. When our ancestors died and left their body, which body itself was later cremated and was, therefore, out of our sight, those whom we refer to as our ancestor come to be related with our memories of the ancestor's gross body, which was in any case impermanent, but our memories relating to that body, and the thoughts which were being experienced by our mind in relation to that gross body, remained fresh. In all these enterprises, the question or relevancy of the ancestor's Self never comes to our mind. Even now when we think of our ancestor, it is not his Self that is considered but his gross body which comes to our mind.

What is true of our ancestor is equally true about our own body and the Self. We never consider our Self to be our true nature or true existence but the gross body with all the thoughts, concepts and memories. Herein lies our misery and bondage, which when enquired into, reflected and meditated, becomes the beginning of our redemption.

How then and in what manner does the perception of the mind gets associated with such subjective impressions ? Bhagavan says that whatever state of mind one may be in, the perception of the mind is influenced and shaped by that state. That is, if one is in the waking state (*jagratavastha*), the mind perceives outwardly through the gross body with the gross organs of perception the gross subjective names and forms; in dream state (*svapnavastha*) the mind perceives internally through the mental or psychic body, the mental creations in their manifold forms and names; in the deep dreamless state (*sushupti*), since there is no identification of the mind with the body, there is no active subjective perceptions. Similarly in the transcendental state (*Turiyavastha*) the pure Self remains in identity with its own Self or the Supreme Brahman, which places the man in harmony with everything. There being no awareness of the body or of the thoughts, concepts, hopes and aspirations, which are but the modifications of the mind. One experiences the bliss of the Self and Brahman because apart from the Self and Brahman there is nothing else in existence.

If one desires peace of mind and contentment in heart, then one should eliminate the relationships which the Mind creates in association with the gross body and its organs of perception and of actions, which give the erroneous picture of the empirical world. As Bhagavan puts it: When the mind is in contact with a pleasant experience or memory thereof or when the mind is free from unpleasant experience or memory thereof, we say there is happiness. The contrary feeling is equally true. Such happiness is thus relative. The world we perceive is the world of our mind, of our thoughts, of our hopes, of our aspirations, of misery and of disappointments. Thus we become what our mind chooses us to be come.

The human being, however, wants absolute as well as permanent happiness and not relative happiness which is dependent on the things which are external to himself. He does not desire to be happy because his senses, his thoughts, his desires choose to be happy. He wants to be happy because he wants to be happy independent of or inspite of these external influencing senses. But then, the source of happiness does not reside in external objects but internally in the Heart. Perfect happiness and peace is the nature of the Self. Bliss, therefore, is Brahman.

In Viveka Chudamani, while explaining the five sheaths covering the Self, the sheath of food, of the breath, of the intellect, of the consciousness and of the bliss, Sri Shankra suggests that human being is not aware of the State of Bliss because of the progressively grosser sheaths cover the Self. Once these sheaths are removed one by one, as one would remove the petals of the onion, the Self realises the Blissful State which is of Pure Existence, Brahman.

Taittitiya Upanishad is almost lyrical of this blissful state. "He who is here in the person and he who is yonder in the sun, he is one. He who knows this, on departing from this world, transcending on to the self which consists of food, transcending on to the self which consists of life, transcending on to the self which consists of mind, transcending on to the self which consists of understanding, transcending on to the self which consists of bliss, goes up and down these worlds, eating food he desires, assuming the form he desires. He sits singing the chant: Oh Wonderful, Oh Wonderful, Oh Wonderful" (III.10.5).

Thus, when man speaks of 'I' and 'mine' in the empirical world, he is still in the realm of all those relationships which have been created by the Mind and associated with the body. The moment the Self makes its habitation in the physical body, it acquires impressions from the senses, which create concepts in the mind, which in turn create the ego in relation to the body. Starting with my body, my parents, my wife and my children, my house, my possessions, my society, my nation etc. he continues in creating an alter-image of his Self during the entire existence of the body till it is destroyed or dies. When the body dies the real 'I' or the Self does not die therefore it does not come to be cremated; it is only the body which is cremated.

However, even after the dis-association of the Self with the body, people will continue to associate the Self with the thoughts and the body and they will not take cognisance of the 'I' or the Self independent of the body. In fact one is not at all concerned with the associations which the Self had prior to its emergence in the body or after the divergence with the body. Their association is entirely with the particular gross body and all the thoughts, memories of the Mind which go along with that.

Therefore, it become all the more important for us to be fully aware of the 'I' to which the thoughts, concepts, the memories have given an erroneous sense of identity.

IV

In one sense, 'I' or the Self is really nothing new to be enquired into, to be known or to be experienced. Every one knows that it exists ! 'I exist' is one continuous and constant awareness of the Self by a human being during his entire lifetime, whether he is in wakeful state, dream state, dreamless state. There is no stage when one can say 'I' does not exist and a person is not aware of it. Even if we are not aware or do not take cognisance of it, 'I' nevertheless exists. Therefore, there is nothing new to be aware of. Then why is the enquiry about 'I' ?

In reply to Paul Brunton, Bhagavan had in fact clarified: "The first and the foremost of all thoughts, the primeval thought in the mind of every man, is the thought of 'I'. It is only after the birth of this thought that any other thought can arise at all. It is only after the first personal pronoun, 'I' has arisen in the mind that the second personal pronoun, 'you' can make appearance. If you could mentally follow the 'I' thread until it leads you to its source, you would discover that just as it is the first thought to appear, so it is also the last one to disappear. This is matter which can be experienced."

Therefore, the question of enquiring 'Who am I ?' really arises when the question of searching the source of the erroneous 'I' or the 'I' thought arises. Our search, therefore, in reality is the search as well as the denial of the thing which is not 'I'. In that very denial of erroneous 'I', does the realisation of the Real 'I' comes about. This appears like a contradiction but it is not really so.

One should not commence one's enquiry by questioning consciously of such thoughts like : 'I am not the body etc.'. Seeking the source of 'I', itself leads one to severance of all other thoughts. Every moment one should refuse to give scope to other thoughts to arise but concentrate one's attention fixed on finding out the source from which the 'I' thought rises. For instance, one should enquire (even as each thought arises) to whom such thought arises, then that very question will have its answer in its own embryo. If the answer is 'I get the thought' then one should further enquire, who is this 'I' that gets the thought and where is its origin. Being aware of the Truth means being conscious of such awareness not merely the destruction of that which is not the truth. Illumination does not mean destruction of Darkness but being aware of the Light. There is nothing that can be called Darkness; Darkness is the absence of Light.

Evolution, in the true sense of Divine Intent, involves destruction as essential a phase as the creation. Death is the price which one is required to pay for being aware of the palpable presence of the Divinity within oneself and the continuance of the Values of life. Death of the thoughts and concepts is as essential as the death of the body in the evolution of the Self in the process of enquiry. Then there will never ever be the fear that WE may 'die', because every moment one breathes and the heart beats its every beat, our body dies and our thoughts lose their vibrancy and freshness of the Present Moment.

Thus in the enquiry 'Who am I ?', the 'I' is the ego. Trying to trace it and find its source, one will realise that it has no separate or independent existence, even as Darkness has no independent existence. When the real 'I' ceases to be known this erroneous 'I' comes in the front. In other words, the conventional 'I', which is the ego does not exist on its support. It needs the thoughts, the concepts, the memories as prop.

Therefore, the real question and the enquiry should be directed how this erroneous 'I' the ego comes about. What is the source or the origin of this ego ? For this purpose one need not imagine that one is not the body which bears such or such description, with such or such name etc. There is the need only to have an awareness that this body is not the 'I' and it does represent the true nature of one's Self. 'I', which is the real Self, exists as it always did. It is nothing new to be created or to be searched and found. Because it is real and not mere imagination.

A visitor once remarked about the pain in the world. A man is hungry. It is physical reality. It is very real to him. Is one to call it a dream or Maya and remain unmoved or unconcerned by such pain?

Maharishi replied him: From the point of view of *JNANA* or the reality, the hunger or the pain you speak of is certainly a dream, *Maya*, as is the world, of which the hunger or the pain is an infinitesimal part. In your dream also, you experience hunger. You also see others suffering from hunger. You see pain in dreams also and are moved by pity. You feed others whom you find suffering from hunger. So long as the dream lasted, all the pains, hunger and the pity you felt were quite as real, as now you consider the pain you see in the world around you. But just as when you woke up from the sleep you realised that the pain in the dream was unreal, you will also realise when you become a Jnani, a man of wisdom that even the hunger and the pain which you felt when you are in the wakeful state is also not real but the response of your mind to the stimuli of the senses of the Gross body.

Similarly you might have eaten full and gone to sleep.

Yet you may feel very hungry in your sleep. You dream that you are working hard and long in the hot sun, and that you are perspiring, tired, hungry and want to rest. Yet when you wake up you will find that you have not stirred at all out of your bed. But all this is not to say that while you were in the dream, you can act as if the pain you feel in the dream state was not real. The hunger in the dream was as real to you as was your hunger in wakeful state. The hunger has to be assuaged by taking the food in the dream as we do when we are awake. The people whom you found in the dream hungry had to be provided with food in the dream as you would surely do for those whom you find hungry in the wakeful state. You should never mix up these two states - the dream and the waking state.

Till one transcends the shackles of Samsara and the Maya, the world we see would mot disappear. It's meaning and relevance ever remain to the person who is attached to his body and the senses. Till one reaches the state of *JNANA* and is delivered from the web of this *MAYA*, one must accept all these things as really existing, but with a sense quite different from the present erroneous attachment and importance. All must be accepted as the Self and of the nature of Godhead, the things of the dream as well as the things of the waking state.

Bhagavan insists that it is possible for us, while we live our empirical life, to be conscious of our Self and its seeming Silence in our empirical life. Even while living this life of appearances, we can still live the life of the nature. Only when we position ourself in the timeless state of being that Time, Space and the Events fall away from us and begin to appear as mere dreams sequences. If we can separate ourselves from our waking state as we do separate ourselves from the dream state, then we will really be aware of the Reality.

Till such state arrives, we must do social service by relieving sufferings wherever we see it. But even then we must not do it with ahankara, i.e. with the sense 'I am the doer', but with the feeling 'I am the Lord's tool'...We must help the man as a means of worshipping God in that man. All such services are in fact to the Self in the body, not for the body as such. Consequently, we are not helping anybody else, but only helping our own Self. This is what Yajnavalkya means when he says: *"na are sarvasya kamaya sarvam priyam bhavati, atmanastu kamaya sarvam priyam bhavati"* (Brihad Aranyak Up.II.4.5).

According to Sri Ramana we always tend to have misconception about our role in the world due to the wrong identification about our Self. We live in two worlds with which we are not able to identify ourselves. The first world is the world of the waking state. The moment we wake up, the primeval feeling of 'I' arises in our mind but that 'I' is not the real 'I' but collection of the responses and impressions which the mind has stored through the senses. This collected mass of impressions create an arche type, which is the EGO which identifies these impressions with the body. It comes to believe that the body represents the 'I' along with all the mental impressions, because the body with the medium of senses gets associated with all the impressions on the mind. But the 'I' is independent of these mental impressions.

In the Dream state, the body does not play any part. In that state a separate form of body is created by the mind with which all the impressions of the dream state get associated. The body in the dream state is as distinct and as real as the body in the wakeful state. It has a great resemblance with the body of the waking state. These Ego-centered-bodies though distinct and independent of each other, appear to give the impressions of continuity, a close and seeming relationship between the two states.

Independent of these two states, the 'I' also exists in the dreamless state as well as in the transcendental state without being associated with the body. But in these two latter states the Ego-centered body is not conscious of itself and the mind is silent. But none the less the real 'I', the Self continues to exist, giving certainty to the fact that the real 'I' is not the Ego-centered body. In all these four states, there is the unbroken and continuing thread of the real 'I' which is the Self.

Sri Ramana concludes that if the human being becomes at all aware of this Real 'I', which is not constrained by the Ego-centered body, then it would only be in the blissful state, turiyavastha, when the impressions which the mind receives in the wakeful and the dream states do not interfere with the Self.

He therefore suggests that our enquiry should be in the four stages, *DEHAM, NAHAM, KOHAM, SOHAM.* i.e. 1) The Body. 2) 'I' am not that body. 3) Who, then am 'I'? 4) 'I' am , verily, THAT. In the first stage, it is explained what is *DEHAM*, the body consists of. In the second stage, it is established '*NAHAM*', i.e. 'I' am not that body. In the third stage the enquiry centers around *KOHAM*, then who am I ? And finally after enquiry one comes to be aware that *SOHAM*, i.e., I am That, the Brahman. *Aham Brahmasmi*, as the Upanishads declare. Thus if one inquires whence this 'I' springs and realises that it is That One, which abides in the heart, then the fulfillment of the enquiry comes about and the persons is freed from the torments of the flesh.

To another devotee he explained the significance of 'I' as follows. 'I exist' is the only permanent, self evident experience of every one. Nothing else is self evident (*pratyaksha*) as 'I am'. What people consider as self-evident in normal life, i.e. the experiences which they get through the senses, are far from being self evident. The Self alone is

That. *Pratyaksha* is another name for the Self. Therefore, to do Self analysis and to be in the state of 'I am' is the non-dual state of Awareness. Thus 'I am' is the Reality. 'I am THIS or THAT' is unreal because it presumes separate status for 'I' and 'That'. 'I am' alone is the TRUTH, another name for Self. 'I am God' is not true.

One of the devotees remarked. The Upanishads themselves have said 'I am Brahman'. To this Bhagavan clarified, That is not how the text is to be understood. It simply means, Brahman exists as 'I' and not 'I am Brahman...' 'I' and Brahman are not separate. The emphasis should be on Brahman and not the Self, which is only the reflection of the original.

Our concentration should be on the purpose of enquiry in the Self, not as a goal to be achieved or a state of BECOMING but as a state of BEING. He further clarified that the Self or Atman is always as it is. There is no such thing as attaining it. All that is necessary is to be aware of the veil which obscures the 'I', the Self from Brahman, and give up considering the Ego which is the non-self, as the Self, the unreal as the Real. When we give up such erroneous identification of our Self with the body, the Self alone remains.

The importance of the need to enquire 'Who am I' or the source of 'I' is highlighted extensively by Sri Ramana to another devotee who had asked him about the nature of Self Realisation? Possibly, the devotee was impressed by the technological and scientific advances which were taking place with more emphasis on the intellect of the man and the materials of the world. These so-called modern intellectuals were give to desired the belief in God of Self. Those who believe in religion, gods and other worlds were psychopaths.

Sri Ramana was never given to argue fruitlessly and never encouraged unnecessary discussions, since they are not conducive to the knowledge of the Truth. He would curtly dissuade such inane arguments. He would say, never mind what the materialists or others say; and don't even bother about Self or God. But do you exist or not? What is your idea about yourself? What do you mean when you utter the word 'I'?

Many devotees obviously would not understand Sri Ramana's such counter questions. Because they had not come to him for any intellectual encounters. They had come for answers and clarifications and if possible, then for some quick relief. Some would meekly admit that they did understand that 'I' has to do with something within the body and it is different from body. But this intellectual understanding did not make them aware of the Lord within or gave any relief from the torments of the world. Thereupon Bhagavan would continue like a compassionate teacher towards a newly introduced student. You concede, he would say, that 'I' is not the body but something within the body. See whether it arises and disappears, and whether it is always present. You will agree that there is an 'I' which rises up as soon as one wakes up, sees the body, the world and all else, and cease to exist when one sleeps. There is another 'I' which exists apart from and independent of the body, and which alone is, when the body and the world does no longer exist, as in the case of sleep. In such situation, one should ask for oneself whether the same 'I' of which he was aware in the walking state, exists or not, during sleep as well as during the other states. One should reason out whether there could be two 'I's ? One in the waking state and the other in dream and other states. Only on such enquiry one will realise that the 'I' is always the same.

Now, then, which can be the Real One - the 'I' which comes and goes, or the 'I' which always abides? The crux of the enquiry is the realisation is that the 'I' which comes and goes is the ego, influenced by the sense during each of the states, whereas the 'I' which ever is, is the Self. Then you will be aware that you are the Self. This is called Realisation. Self Realisation is not a state which is foreign to oneself, which is far from oneself, and which has to be reached by one. One is always in that state. The only error which the human being does is that he forgets that he is the Self, which is unattached and ever blissful, and identifies himself with the ego, which is shaped by the sense contacts and influenced by the mind with all its thoughts, concepts, ideas etc. To cease to identify oneself with the mind, is all that is required. The human being has identified oneself with the non-self for such a long time that he finds it difficult to accept that there is something called his own unalloyed, pure, blissful Self. Freeing oneself from erroneous identification with the non-Self is what is called deliverance or Self Realisation.

Sri Ramana's words are like elixir to the enquirer, because he becomes aware of the real 'I' the Self within which is similar to the Lord, the Brahman, if he divests himself of the wrong identifications and becomes receptive and surrenders to his Self, which is the Source, Real and Eternal. The mind is cramped with unessential garbage. If the clear waters of the stream are desired to be enjoyed then the moss that has gathered in the Mind needs to be cleared. It needs to be emptied and the receplacle, the Mind, needs to cleaned and kept pure and shining, so that the essential nature of the Self can shines in its natural brightness.

The cleansing of the mind, however, is not a physical step but the spiritual step before one seeks to walk on the Path to Perfection. On this journey, there are no goal to be reached and attained therefore no physical steps to be tread. It is journey without physical movements but with peaceful abidance in one's own Self. The cleansing the mind of the thoughts as they arise, is itself one's sadhana to be in a state of mind that is free of distractions.

Sri Ramana repeatedly assures that there is no goal to be reached. There is nothing to be achieved. There is nothing like BECOMING something other than what you essentially are. You are essentially the Self. You exist always. Nothing more can be predicated of the Self than that it EXISTS. Therefore BEING your own Self is being God, as it were. BEING your own Self is realising the Truth. Seeing is BEING. How can you BEING the Self itself can hope to see it as if it is other that You ! It is something similar to the person who, even while standing in the Ramanashrama was asking how to reach Ramanashram. There are many ways to reach Ramanashrama and each one should find the mode which is the best suited to his sva-bhava.

Self is nothing other than 'BE-ING', not being this or that. It is simple case of BEING. BE...and there is the end of Ignorance. Everyone is aware of his Self clearly and with certainty. Everyone knows that he exists. But he is not aware the significance of such existence or what it means to BE. The BE-ING is the Self. 'I am' is the name of God. Sri Ramana used to say repeatedly that of all the definitions of God, none is more dramatically put that the Biblical statement 'I AM THAT I AM'. There are also other statements such as '*Brahmaiv aham*', '*Aham Brahmasmi*' and '*Soham*'. But none is so direct as the name *JEHOVAH* = I AM. The Absolute Being is, WHAT IS. It is the Self. It is God. Knowing the Self, the God is known.

Bliss is not something to be acquired. On the contrary each person is always the Bliss. The desire to become something is born out of one's sense of incompleteness. To whom is the sense of incompleteness ? This problem is also to enquired. In deep sleep every one is blissful. In the wakeful state one does not feel so. What has happened in the intervening periods of the state of bliss and no-bliss? What is it that makes a person, blissful in one state and not blissful in the other ? On enquiry it will be seen that it is the Ego that interferes with. When one seeks the source of this ego, one will find that the ego ceases to exist seen one proceeds in his enquiry. There is no room of for ego which is the product of *Tamas*, (obscurity) on the mind.

The Teacher clarifies, directs, advises, counsels. Then, after all these clarifications are given, the steps are to be taken, the efforts are to be made by the individual himself. The Teacher remains only as the sign-post. As Bhagavan puts it, for those who, because of the various influences on their minds, are deluded into believing that they are the bodies, a Guru and *Sadhana* are necessary to get rid of that delusion.

What, then, is the *Sadhana*, what is the need for a Guru. How does Guru influences or guides the aspirant are all the questions which arise in the mind of the aspirant. This, then, becomes the further step in the Enquiry, which we will ask Sri Ramana outwardly and our own Self internally.

V

Having received clarifications in the true nature of the Reality and the substance of Realisation, we will now approach Sri Ramana for information in the modalities of *Sadhana*. Information, it surely would be. But if it is not followed by practice, effort of our own, then all the instructions will be infructious. Sri Ramana did not and in fact was reluctant to initiate any one formally to Sadhana in the traditional sense of the word. Even though he has spoken the importance of having a Guru more than once, he himself was reluctant to don the role of a Guru in the traditional manner. Therefore, he had devotees but no disciples. Nevertheless the requirement of Guru and Sadhana was given its due importance. But he could not see himself as the traditional Acharya, having number of disciple being initiated and instructed by him. Even though his approach to Truth was intellectual and that of the man of wisdom He had not visualise himself a preacher of Truth based on theoretical or philosophical tenets. Nor had he come to establish a tradition or a parampara. He had nothing of his own to talk about nor anything which is to be accepted from him as Gospel Truth. He had no dogma, no Path, nor any set of beliefs to be accepted or rituals to be followed. He was neither a dialectician nor a commentator of the Truth 'seen' by the ancient Seers. He was a seer himself having 'seen' Truth all by himself. He himself had no Guru in the conventional sense nor any particular sadhana was laid down for him.

Therefore, he too believed in role for him as a Guru or as a Teacher or any theory to be propounded. He wanted others to see Truth as even he had seen it. He said he had been aware of Truth through constant enquiry in the nature of 'I' and he wanted others to accept that manner to search the Truth, and search it by themselves.

Therefore, he did neither recommend any formal sadhana nor even accepting him as the Guru. *Sadhana*, in the conventional sense, as understood by him was explained by him. When he himself was asked about the *Sadhana* which he had performed, he remarked: *Sadhana*? *Sadhana* for what purpose ? What is there anything particular about performing *Sadhana* ? Sitting quiet itself is *Sadhana.* He would say that he used to sit quietly always. He used to close his eyes then; now he keeps them open. That is all the difference. What is now, was also earlier. What was there then, is also here now. *Sadhana* is necessary only if there is a thing other than 'I', the Self. *Sadhana* is required only for one who does not look towards the Self which is permanent, but is deluded by looking at the body etc. which are transitory and delusive; but not for one who sees the Self and does not see anything else different. And what else is *Sadhana* meant for? To keep the Mind restrained of the thought waves is *Sadhana*. If you could keep them quiet when you are in crowd then there is no reason for you to go to the jungles. Mental Peace is the state of mind, not the product of the situation.

When some one remarked whether such exalted state of mind, and of existence, which is natural and possible for exceptional persons like Sri Ramana, would be possible for ordinary people, without conventional *Sadhana*, recommended and practiced over the centuries.

To this Sri Ramana assured without any hesitation. Certainly *Sadhana* is necessary. But then what purpose is that *Sadhana* required for ? The Self is there all the times and all places. So there is no need to try and get it from some one or from somewhere else. Sadhana is only to get rid of the misconceptions about the body and to be aware of its relation with the Self, since these come in the way of realisation. This mind gets deluded only when one thinks this gross world is Real, instead of being aware of the Self, which alone is Real. *Sadhana* is effort, perseverance to get rid of this illusion. In other words, why should there be *Sadhana* for the Self to be aware of its own Self ?

The crux of the matter is to be aware of the distinct nature of the real and the unreal. '*nityaanitya viveka*' as Sri Shankara would put it. The discrimination between the things which hinder the realisation of the true nature of the Self and the things which aid, help, assist to be freed from these hindrances, is Sadhana. In fact the moment one becomes aware of the hindrances, he becomes as it were, without any further efforts, aware of the Reality which is the Self.

Sri Ramana has made a keen distinction here between Sadhana for "Realisation" and the *Sadhana* for removal of the illusions of the empirical world. While for the former there is no need of *Sadhana* or a Guru, for the latter the grace or the guidance of the Guru, and also the company of the saints, study of the scriptures, meditation and all the rest constitute *Sadhana* and are essential and useful. They are only aids, the means not the ends to cultivated, nurtured and to be dwelled upon.

While "Realisation" of the Self is an individual endeavour, the removal of the erroneous idea that the ego or the body is 'I', could be supportive activity of the Teacher, the scriptures, the company of noble minded people.

Sri Ramana realises that Guru and *Sadhana* are needed for the one who has not yet started the enquiry into his Self, the 'I'. He used to say that the teachings, lectures, meditations precede the grace of the Guru, which gives consummation to the intellectual knowledge, because the Grace is Illumination of the intellect and it has to be direct and personal. Realisation is the primary and the essential cause. All else is secondary.

Even then, Self transcends intellect and, therefore, intellect should cease to exist before the Self could be realised.

Unless one knows the approach intellectually, how can one practice it ? Knowing intellectually about the nature of the Self one should stop there. Intellectual knowledge has to be transformed in to intuitive awareness. For this, the spark of the Guru's Grace, which is nothing other than Divine Intervention, is required to consummate. Reading a book on Yoga and mastering its techniques does not make one a Yogi. Even Patanjala Yoga, devotion to and Divine grace is accepted as an aid for concentration. Mere book learning is not of any great use. After realisation all intellectual information becomes useless load, a burden to be thrown overboard.

While Sri Ramana puts emphasis on the grace of Guru as a sine qua non for realising Self, he is emphatic that the Guru need not be in human form. The Guru comes in any form. Even Self itself becomes the Guru, as it was in the case of Sri Ramana himself. Who is a Master, he would ask. He is the Self after all. In fact, the human form of the Guru, ceases to have relevance in his spiritual development after some time, when the aspirant looks within and his Self itself takes up the role. Every event presents to itself for enquiry by the internal Self and solution also come from within. The instance of Sri Dattatrya is the classic example, who had twenty four Gurus, human as well as non-human, animate as well as inanimate. The Lord, the Supreme Self takes the role of

Guru either as the Self in an external gross form or as the Self in one's internal subtle Self. And they are all identical since both of them source their power from the Lord Himself. Supreme Lord is the original and Primal Teacher.

How then does one seek a qualified Guru suitable for one's needs ? How does one to know that he has not unknowingly fallen in the hands of spurious Guru, who instead of guiding the aspirant on the right path, would take him for a ride ? It has been the experience of so many people who have, in the moment of emotional stress, accepted some one as Guru, who had gift of gab, and mastery over speech, only to rue in leisure ! Sri Shankara declares in Viveka Chudamani that "Just as the beauty of the musical instrument and the expertise of the musician could be the source of pleasure but would not bestow any empire, similarly the learned man's mastery over speech, flow of words, capacity of explaining the scriptures or knowledge would surely be source of pleasure, not of deliverance."

Sri Ramanahadalso similar advise. He had great faith on individual effort and endeavour. He would commend that if one goes on working with the light available, the one is sure to meet the Master, as the Master himself will be seeking the aspirant. But, Ishta Devata and Guru are only aids - very powerful aids on this path. But an aid to be effective requires individual effort also, which is a sine qua non. It is for the person to see the Sun. Can spectacles and the Sun see for you, he would ask ? The Guru or the God are like the spectacles. One has to see one's own true nature by his own Self. Not much assistance is required for doing that !

Many of the visitors would ask questions without possibly knowing the immense significance which they contain for one who is intent of realisation. One of the visitor wanted to know, why was it said that knowledge born of hearing is not firm, whereas that born of contemplation is firm ? For Sri Ramana the question was important not the questioner. He conceded that it is generally accepted that hearsay knowledge (*paroksha*) is not firm whereas the knowledge born of one's own realisation (*aparoksha*) is firm. It is also said that hearing helps the intellectual understanding of Truth, but meditation makes that understanding clear, and finally reflection and meditation brings about realisation of the Truth. Further, all knowledge is not firm; it becomes firm only it becomes personal experience and intimate as the gooseberry in the hollow of one's palm.

There are those who affirm that hearing alone will be sufficient; because a qualified person who had, perhaps in previous lives, equipped himself with the necessary intellectual ground knowledge, realises in this life as soon as he hears the Truth conveyed to him even once, whereas the persons not so qualified must pass through the stages and many lives before realising the Truth.

Even assuming that the grace of the Guru is precondition for realisation of Self, then one may wonder how this grace can be availed of. To this Sri Ramana assures that Guru's grace is always there. As Sri Shankara said, "*ayam svabhavah svatah eva yat parashramaapanodavapramaanam mahathmanaam*". One imagines Grace to be something, somewhere high up in the sky, far away, and has to descend down on the aspirants as Sun shine or the rains. In fact, it is already inside the person, inside the heart and the moment (by any of the methods) one causes the mental waves subside or merge in its source, the Grace rushes forth, sprouting as spring, from within the person. The Grace is Brahman, and therefore Brahman is said to have derived from the root 'Brh' - to grow, to burst forth.

His constant refrain was that the Lord's grace is the ceaseless flow of luminosity. There is no time when it does not flow. But only those who have are receptive (*Shraddhavan*) or the qualified (*Adhikari*), can receive it. Devotion and commitment is a condition precedent, not for the flow of the Grace, but for the communion and consummation of the Grace. Remembering God itself is the indication that Lord's Grace has already been flowing. The Lord is by nature the Grace. It is by God's grace that you think of God.

Shraddha (receptivity) in oneself is the same as having *Shraddha* in the Lord. Because approach to the Lord has to be made internally and not externally. But to have access to the inward dwelling place of the Lord, one has to be pure in mind and in heart. Because, *Shraddha* does not mean having intellectual faith or belief in some persons words, or in some creed or dogma, but being receptive to the clarity which flows from the unencumbered pure mind. The passage to the heart invariably passes through the Mind.

Sri Ramana had an effective manner of making a point clear to the aspirant. When some one asked him, how long is a Guru necessary for Self Realisation? He replied, Guru is necessary so long as there is *LAGHU*. (He used here pun on the word GURU = heavy and LAGHU=light). Laghu is due to the restriction imposed on the Self due to erroneous identifications. God, on being worshipped, bestows steadiness to devotion, which in turn leads to surrender. On the devotee surrendering, the God shows his Grace by manifesting as Guru. The Guru, otherwise God, guides the Devotee, saying that God is in your own Self and He is, verily, the Self. This leads to introspection, reflection and finally to Realisation. Consistent effort is necessary for reaching the state of realisation.

In Katha Upanishad, *Yama* tells Nachiketa that "Proper and the Pleasant approach the *Jiva*. The wise one (*dhirah*) pondering over both, discriminates. The wise chooses only the Proper in preference to the Pleasant. (But) the man of little understanding, preferring worldly well being, chooses the Pleasant" (I.2.2). Men are always faced with insurmountable problems in life. On such occasions, the man either looks to the things which might make him forget these miseries by resorting to alcohol or he might look unto the Lord to release from the effects of these miseries. The moment when the wise one prefers the Proper in place of the Pleasant or prefers the Lord in place of the alcohol etc., the Grace of the Lord may be said to be flowing. Thus both the Pleasant and the Proper is within the reach of the human being; so is the Grace of the Lord.

However one should have consistency in one's approach to Sadhana. Effort toward such consistency is called *UPASANA*. Sri Shankara defines Upasana "as abiding for long on the subject of upasana as prescribed, visualising it and dwelling thereon closely and evenly like the FLOW OF THE OIL. It will be our effort to understand how Bhagavan approaches the subject of Upasana or Sadhana; and that is what we will do next.

VI

It is useful to understand the fundamentals. If we do not agree on the fundamentals and accept them then we are likely to be mislead in our premises. We can accept, for instance, the definition by Sri Shankara of the word Upasana as a working definition. According to him, one should approach the subject of enquiry with a receptive mind, visualise the subject of enquiry, abide therein for a long time, continuously and uninterruptedly like the flow of oil – "Upasanam nama yatha shastram upasyarthasya vishayikarena, sanmipyamupagamya, tailadharavat samanapratyaya-pravahena dirghakale yadasanam".

Sri Ramana himself had said in another context that sadhana is required for one who does not look towards the Self which is permanent but is deluded by looking at the body etc. which are transitory and delusive. Sadhana is not for the one who abides in the Self and therefore, does not see other things as different from himself or from Brahman. Such abidance itself is Sadhana.

Sri Ramana himself did not do any upasana or sadhana in the traditional manner. For him his life itself was upasana and sadhana. When some one asked him long did it take him to realise the Self, he had replied thus: This question is asked because the name and form are perceived. These are the perceptions consequent to the identification of the 'I' with the gross body. When one is aware of Self and dwells in it, then the question of any external Upasana does not arise at all.

When another one asked whether reading scriptures and books etc. is necessary, he clarified that if one reads the scriptures and books, after realising the Self, the contents become self-evident. If one reads it before realising the Self, one may experience many discrepancies and inconsistencies, because the mystical meaning will not be revealed to him. In fact there is nothing worthwhile that can be known by the aspirant from the scriptures.

What the scriptures do is the awakening of the consciousness of the aspirant towards the Truth which the seers have claimed to be the vision of the Truth. They are more like the record-books which a traveller writes about the strange places he had visited and the things he had seen. By reading these books, the person only gets the information about the things which the traveller had seen, enjoyed and experienced. These books cannot make the reader see, enjoy or experience those places. For that purpose the reader has to travel to those places himself and see, enjoy, experience. It is in this sense that Sri Shankara said the Vedas are only informatory and not mandatory - "Jnapakam hi shastram na tu karakam iti stithih".

But in the case of Self, there is nothing to be realised. Because it is 'nitya shuddha buddha mukta' - the Eternal, the Pure, Awareness and Deliverance. There is no place to be reached, because the Self is here in the very heart of the person. There is nothing new to be gained, because one is always possessed of the Self.

On the other hand one must lose to gain. One must lose his ignorance by 'knowing' and by being aware of one's real nature. One must lose the totality of thoughts which are in mind before the mind can respond to the resonance of the Self within. Effortless and choiceless awareness of one's Self would then one's real nature. One's endeavour, therefore, should be to attain that state of BEING and abide in it. But this cannot be done easily because the age old vasanas, the sense-bound attachments on the human mind have completely influenced and bound the Mind. These shackles are first required to be broken and uprooted completely. Blissful awareness is reached not after thinking about intellectually the hindrances to the clarity of the mind, but by removing the hindrances.

The reflection and meditation helps one to consider how the thoughts arise in mind. Observing them as they arise, leads one to the source of those thoughts and that very realisation will make the new thoughts drop from arising. This quietens the mental process and the modifications to which our over-active mind is to respond and react in response to every thoughts as it arises.

Sri Ramana removed certain misconceptions from people's mind regarding taking up the enquiry in the nature of the Self, or enquiring "Who am I ?" For taking up such enquiry, people need not give up family life and adopting sanyas. This is not a pre- condition. When some one asked how does a 'grihastha' (householder) fare in the scheme of liberation, he queried; why should one think oneself as 'grihastha' ? If one goes on thinking himself as sanyasi that very thought, that he is a sanyasi, will continue to pursue and haunt him. Whether one continues in the house hold, or renounce it and go to the forest or the hills, his mind will continue to remain with him. Therefore it is immaterial to what stages one belongs to. Vasishtha, Atri, Yajnavalkya were born as householders, Janaka was born a King and realised in their as householders or kings.

As mentioned in Vedanta Desika "*tvam chet praseedasi tavasmi sameepatschet, tvayee astir bhaktir anagha kari-Shailanatha, samsrijyate yadi cha daasajanas tvadeeyah, samsara esha bhagavan apavarga eva*" – O Lord, if you are gracious, if I am by your side, if there is in me pure devotion, if I am in the company of those who are your servants, then this *samsara*, verily, is itself the sàlvation. After realisation the realised souls decide to remain out of compassion for men and in order to help them also to cross over.

The ego, the ahamkara, is the source of thoughts. It creates the body with association of the thoughts and his empirical world. This is what makes him think himself to be a grihastha and binds him to this samsara. If one considers that by deserting one's family and one's present environment he renounces the family and the world, it would be his misconception. That will only result in substituting the idea of '*sanyasi*' for '*grihastha*' and the environment of the forest for that of the household. But the mental obstacles will always be there and may even increase or aggravate in the new surroundings due to the strange environment.

The change in the environment would therefore not be helpful by itself. *Vairagya* is not running away from Life. It is the state of mind which rejects the influences and attachments which the life projects to the mind and the responses which the mind in turn throws out. The obstacles, therefore, are the thoughts that arise in the mind. This obstacles should be surmounted whether at home or in the forest. The garbage that is collected in mind should be thrown, not the vessel in which the garbage was collected.

The mind, by its very nature, is restless. It is more mobile than even the wind. Begin liberating it from its restlessness; give it peace; make it free from distractions; train it to look inward; make it abide in the core of your heart wherein dwells the Self, the Lord. Achieve this by practice. Make this a habit. This is done by diverting the mind from the influences of the external world and reverting it within the Self. This will enable not only to remove the existing obstacles but also from gathering new obstacles to the peace of mind.

One of the thing which Sri Ramana recommended for peace of mind and removal of the obstacles was cultivation of solitude in mind. Even here Sri Ramana had different interpretation about solitude. In the present age where the forces of Samsara assail from all the sides, the word 'solitude' has to be redefined. Solitude is not being in a solitary place far from maddening crowd, but by being far from the influences which they cause. Solitude is the state of the mind not of physical presence, he said. One might be in the thick of the world and yet maintain the serenity of mind; such a one is in solitude. Another one may stay in a forest and still be unable to keep his mind under control. Various thoughts would continue to well up in his mind. He cannot be said to be in solitude. Solitude is the function of the mind. A man attached to desire cannot be in solitude wherever he may be; a detached man is always in solitude.

Sri Ramana recommends meditation, for restraining the restlessness of the mind and to regain its peaceful disposition. External contact - contact with objects other than the mind itself - makes the mind restless. *Vairagya* is not forceful renunciation of the external objects or the things which are not conducive to bring the mind at rest, but intelligent rejection of the influence of the external objects. Loss of interest in all those objects, which are of the nature of non-Self, is (*vairagya*). In one respect, even ideation of a personal God, which is not the result consequent to realisation but the mental or psychological inducement as an aid to meditation may become an impediment and may have to be brushed aside from the spiritual path. This is the first step. Then would introspection, analysis, discrimination and concentration follow. They are charecterised by restrain and not the control of external senses, internal faculties, etc. ending in samadhi, which is evenness of mind. Control is not natural act, what is controlled can as well come up with renewed force. What is restrained may eventually cease to exist.

Reflection over and an examination of the ephemeral nature of external phenomenon leads helps restraining the external objects and their influences and ultimately to vairagya. Enquiry (*vichara*) is the first and foremost step to be taken. When *vichara* continues automatically and continuously, it will see the impermanence and, therefore, the futility of and aversion to wealth, fame, ease, pleasure etc. The things which depend on outside factors for acquisition and preservation, should be denied first. Then the 'I' thought becomes clearer for inspection.

The source of 'I' is the heart, the final goal. If, however, the aspirant is not temperamentally suited to vichara-marga, the introspective analytical method, then he must develop *Bhakti* (devotion) to an ideal - may be God, Guru, humanity in general, ethical laws or even an idea of beauty. When one of these takes possession of the individual, other attachments become weaker, i.e. dispassion develops. Attachment for the ideal grows automatically and simultaneously and finally holds the attention. Thus 'ekagrata' concentration grows slowly and imperceptibly, with or without visions and direct aids. But care should be taken, lest the ideal may dominate the process of enquiry to the detriment of the purpose of enquiry.

Sri Ramana used to say that many paths lead to Ramanashram.

In the absence of inquiry or devotion, *pranayama*, restraint of breath may be tried. This is known as Yoga-Marga. If life is endangered the entire interest of the man centres around that one point, the saving of his life. If the breath is held, the mind cannot afford to and does not jump from point to point - external objects. Thus there is rest for the mind so long as breath is controlled. All attention is turned towards breath and its regulation, interest in other matters is temporarily lost.

Mind is disturbed when breath is irregular. Similarly, passions are aroused when breath is irregular, whereas the mind is calm and happy when the breathing is slow and regular. Peace of mind gives rise to happiness not to the pleasures. Pleasures have origin in the stimuli of the gross senses, while happiness is the quality and the state of the mind.

If these are not possible then Sri Ramana suggests *Karma-marga*, the Way of Action for the aspirants, so that universal concern may divert his mind from personal concern, and thereby make him see the Lord in every thing he doe. '*Jana-seva*' is '*Janardana-seva*'.

Thus there is no one particular path to be adopted. Whichever path suits one's aptitude, attitude, personality for restraining the distracted mind, that one should be considered as the most suitable. Even regulating the life style by getting up at a fixed hour, bathing in sacred tanks or rivers, performing Japa, observing rituals etc. may help people by directing the mind to the ultimate goal, i.e. the Enquiry of the Self. Who is it that wakes up, takes baths, performs Japas and the rituals. It is surely not the body. It must then be the 'I' which is the energy within which prompts and makes the body perform the actions which it intends. Thus, all these methods may ultimately may lead to the enquiry of the 'I' or the Self or the Brahman, by whatever name it may be called.

For Sri Ramana,.there is nothing superior than Enquiry of the source of 'I' or in the question, 'Who am I' because all other methods are only preparatory to this Ultimate Method. Other methods help the mind only to become quiet and serene, so that the Supreme Method, the Enquiry may be taken up. Because Enquiry alone would lead one to Jnana, Wisdom, Awareness. "*na hi jnanena sadrasham pavitram iha vidyate*" says Sri Krishna in Bhagavad Gita (IV.38).

Other than enquiry, there are no other adequate means. If the mind is sought to be controlled through other means then the mind will appear temporarily to be controlled and quiet. But it will again spring up with force, once the control is removed. Through the control of breath, the mind will also be come quiet; but it will be questioned only so long as the breath is controlled. It is beneficial to restrain the Breath wisely and intelligently. Then and in that event the serenity of mind is like to remain for a longer duration. And when breath resumes its course, the mind will also resume but aware of its normal tendency to wander as impelled by vasanas or the residual impressions. Whether in the state of waking or in samadhi, when the mind becomes quiet, the breath is in the state of restraint. Because, then the mind is not forcibly controlled. Breath is the gross form of mind.

Thus, breath restraint is only one of the aid for rendering the mind quiet (manonigraha); it will not destroy the mind (manonasha). Other methods could also be adopted, like meditation on the forms of God, repetition of mantras, restriction on food etc. But they are all the aids for rendering the mind quiet. They do not destroy the Mind; they only influence of the thoughts existing in the mind and divert the attention from the senses to the spiritual aspect of the life.

The rationale behind this remark was further explained by him as under: Whenever one concentrates on whatever centre, there is always the 'I' that concentrates, whereas the object should be to concentrate on the 'I' itself or the source of 'I'. Different people concentrate on different centres, not only the brain and the heart but also the space between the eyebrows, the tip of the nose, the tip of the tongue, the lower most chakra and even external objects. Such concentration leads to some sort of *LAYA*, equanimity, in which one feels certain bliss, but care should be taken to see that one does not lose in this state of *LAYA*, or lose the thought of 'I am' in all this. Because the 'I' is independent of those states and never ceases to exist in all these experiences.

Therefore, in the final analysis enquiry in the source of 'I' alone should be the fundamental basis. Because only on that foundation would true Realisation rest. The thought 'Who am I' will destroy all other thoughts, and, like the stick used for stirring the burning pyre, the thought itself will get burnt to ashes in the end. Then there will be the 'I' nor the process of enquiry. There will only be Self Realisation.

The enquiry in 'I' does not mean discussing the pros and cons of the 'I'or the Self, or dialectical discussion or rationalisation on the opinions or the statements made by earlier Seers. Self enquiry also does not mean arguing or reasoning such as goes on when you say, 'I am not this body, I am not these senses,' etc.; all these may help but they are not what is meant by enquiry. Observing and finding out from where 'I' arises in the body and concentrating your mind on that - that is enquiry.

Invariably people used to ask Sri Ramana from where one should commence the enquiry. He would, then, reply: You talk of 'Where to begin'. There is no beginning and no end. You yourself are the beginning and the end. If you are here and the Self somewhere else, and you have to reach that Self, you may be told to start, how to travel and then how to reach. But the Self is not far from you. It is more closer than the breath you breathe. At the same time it is not meant that you should go on asking 'Who am I'. In that case, that very process of thought will dominate your thinking and the momentum of enquiring process or the capability of the thinking mind will be diminished. All *Japas* are intended, by the use of one thought, the mantra, to exclude all other thoughts. Not to make the words of *Japa* the sole and the final object of concentration. The *Japa* should lead all other thoughts, except the purpose of the mantra, gradually to die. That is the purpose of enquiry.

Our Self is of the nature of *Japa*, being constantly aware of its existence and nature. As the Self is not outside but inside ourselves, one is asked to dive within to be aware. But the fact remains that for some, this method will seem difficult and will not appeal. That is why different methods have been recommended. Each of them should adopt that method which appeals them as the best and easiest. That would then be according to their Guna, svabhava or their capability.

We should stop here and ponder over what has been spoken till now by Sri Ramana. Enough of intellectual clarity and verbal explanations. We must now endeavor, if possible, to delve deep within ourselves and be aware of the Self, the 'I' which Sri Ramana has identified as the source of all our delusions and unhappiness.

To recapitulate what we have intellectually tried to understand, we may go back briefly to the beginning.

VII

Having gone through the spoken words of Sri Ramana as recorded by the Devotees, and having tried intellectually to understand the significance of the salient points as they came to be narrated by different persons, we may now attempt to recapitulate and reconcile them briefly, so that the basic philosophy of Sri Ramana may be evident to us.

Even the endeavour of a life time may not bring us to the state of realising the Self, which Sri Ramana has impressed on us. But at the same time, we can not be said to be aware the extent to which our spiritual life has developed and at what point of realisation we presently are in the process of evolution of our Self.

The lives of the Great Masters, the Saints and Seers have shown us that Realisation has been sudden and unexpected for many of them, even for those whose lives till then had been degenerate and despicable by the moral and ethical standards set by the society. But the fact nevertheless remains that they were not aware of the state and the status to which they had reached in the spiritual quest. For many of them the darkest hour was just prior to illumination of their lives by that Eternal LIGHT. We therefore need not think ourselves less fortunate or evil than any of them, if our intention is clear and purpose is pure.

It is for this reason that prophets have shouted from the roof tops, to arouse us to our destiny. Wake up from the deep slumber, listen to the eternal sound reverberating through the space beyond. "uutishtata jagrata prapya varan nibodhata" - Arise, awake, having attained your boons, be aware of them. This has been the clarion call of the Teachers of Upanishads.

These words were not surely addressed only to Nachiketa or to the select few, but to all the people at large who are intent on redemption. Sri Ramana has been suggested to us as our Mind is, in fact, a wonderful power of the Self. It is the energiser as well as the store house of immense luminosity. Apart from the thoughts that arise therein, there is no such thing as mind. Thought is the nature of mind. Apart from the thoughts there is no independent entity called the world. In deep sleep there are no thoughts and there is no world. In the states of waking and dream, there are thoughts and there is also the world. When the mind comes out of the Self, the world appears. Therefore when the world is luminous (to be real), the Self does not shine. And when the Self is luminous, the world does not shine. The mind always exists subject to and dependent on something gross. It cannot exist independence of thoughts. When thoughts cease to exist, it revels itself in its own blissful luminosity. There is then, what is called realisation.

To the doubting Thomases, Sri Ramana has suggested that one should persistently hold on to the meditation on the Self without yielding to the doubts 'Is it possible or not ?'. Even if one be a great sinner, one should not worry. One should completely renounce the thought 'I am a sinner' and concentrate keenly on the enquiry of the Self, then one would surely succeed. One does not possess two sets of mind - one good and the other evil. The mind is only one. It is the residual impressions that are of two kinds – the auspicious and the inauspicious. When the mind is under the influence of auspicious impressions, it is called good; and when it is under the influence of inauspicious impressions, it is regarded as evil.

Similarly there are no good souls or evil souls. There are only properly guided souls and mis-guided souls. One should not therefore consider hating the evil or loving the noble. The one's who are now noble may have been evil at one time. They have been evil because their minds were obscured by the non-awareness of the Real. Therefore is this adventure of enquiring the source of 'I' and the search for our Self, which alone will release our Self from the bondage in which it has been ensnared.

Let us, therefore, make a determination, which may appear audacious, yet when thought of, may not at all be untenable. We are told that this is not our first or the last of our lives. We are also told that the fact that we are showing inclination towards enquiry in our Self, should itself be an assurance to us that the Grace of the Gods and of the Master has fallen on us. The Lord's Grace does not fall on an unworthy person. Is it not, then given to us to catch, if possible, the ray of the Divine Spark, so that our life be illumined and we may bask in the glory of redemption ?

"Of this Brahman, there is this Teaching: this is as it were, like the lightning which flashes forth or the winking of the eye." says Kena Upanishad. "When the five instruments of knowledge together with the mind cease (from their normal activities) and the intellect itself does not stir, that, they say, is the highest state (pramam gatim)" declares Katha Upanishad. "The wise perceive clearly by wisdom (of the Brahman) the blissful immortal which shines forth. The knot of the heart (is then) cut, all doubts dispelled and deeds terminate, when He is seen, the higher and the lower." assures Mundaka Upanishad.

It is not claimed nor even is it submitted that one can imbibe the teachings of one like Sri Ramana Maharishi unless we are so led towards THE TEACHING by some unseen force. We are told that both the Proper and the

Pleasant approach us. The Wise one chooses the Proper and the dull witted chooses the Pleasant. When the miseries of life assail us, we have two choices before us. We may drown our sorrows by succumbing to the intoxicants or to the pleasures of senses or surrendering ourselves to the mysterious power of our mind and of our Self, which is nothing other than the energy or the effulgence of the Lord for grace and compassion to descend upon us. We have chosen the latter path. We can, then, not surely fail.

Let us, therefore, briefly recapitulate what we have read till now. These premises laid down hereafter may help us crystallising our thoughts and guiding our future.

The First Premise is:

The life which we see and experience, is a mixture of happiness and unhappiness. While the human being prefers enhancement of moments of happiness and diminution of the moments of unhappiness, he does not have apparent control on any of the situations that bring about the state of happiness or unhappiness.

The Second Premise is:

A human being normally looks outside of himself for succor and solace for reducing the moments of unhappiness and for increasing the moments of happiness. These outside agencies may be Gods, Saints, miracle makers, sense based or thought induced solutions and in extreme cases, to drugs, alcohol and such other inducements. Often time, even deserting the field of stresses and strains may be resorted to.

The Third Premise is:

All Seers, Saints, thinkers and men of wisdom have emphasised that these methods do not bring the desired moments of happiness nor do they provide lasting peace to the mind or contentment to the heart. The only solution is to delve deep within, where resides the pure state of Divine Dispensation, in potent form. Sri Ramana Maharishi has not been an exception to this but has certainly been a strong votary of the need to enquire within.

The Fourth Premise is:

Since the solution for our pains and tribulations is within ourselves, we need not go away from ourselves or our environment or from our existing field of action. In fact the field of Righteousness and the field of Action is HERE and NOW, the Dharmakshetra as well as the Kurukshetra. Since our enquiry is directed to the elimination of unhappiness and enhancing the happiness, we should all the more be at the place where these forces of Darkness and of Light have their operations.

The Fifth Premise is:

Since the unhappiness and happiness is the subject matter of our primary enquiry, our attention should be on the Person and not merely on the environment, independent of the person concerned. This leads logically to the Enquiry, WHO IS THIS PERSON, who feels unhappy or happy? In other words, the query would be "Who am I?" who is made to suffer unhappiness and enjoy happiness? The Person and the Purpose of Enquiry both are near one's own Self and one need not go far in search for him.

The Sixth Premise is:

An investigation will show that in common parlance 'I' is taken to be the body and the thought responses. In other words when one refers to oneself, he refers to his body and the associations and circumstances which have been gathered around the gross body influenced and shaped by the thoughts in the mind. But the reality is that the 'I' is in truth neither the body nor the thoughts and impressions gathered by the mind but something other than these. The enquiry in the source and the nature of 'I' or the mind will lead one to a stage when all these misconception vanish and the pure 'I', which is nothing else than what is referred to as SELF, will shine in its own light and brilliance. The Self will be seen as nothing but that state where there is absolutely no 'I' thought. That is called Silence. There, everything becomes the Self and all that is constituted as the world; the Self itself is 'I'; the Self itself is God.

When a man is said to die, what dies is the body and the associations and the circumstances which have gathered around the body, giving rise to phenomenal 'I', which is not the real 'I'. While the body along with the memories and thoughts cease to exist on death of the body, the Self continues to exist in subtle form till it receives a new body and new thoughts. Even for those who are left behind the phenomenal 'I' with the memories and thoughts which the body had, continues to be remembered and the Self no more comes into their consideration.

The Seventh Premise is:

The Self is the Bliss itself, without traces of happiness or unhappiness. The experiences which the senses bring do not affect the Self, which is free from such influences. Without desire, resolve or effort, the Sun rises and in its mere presence the sun-stone emits fire, the lotus blooms, water evaporates, people perform their various functions and then rest. The God (or the Self) has no resolve; no actions to be performed, no gains to be attained. The Action, Karma, does not attach itself to Him. It is similar to the worldly actions not affecting the Sun or the merits and demerits of the other four elements not influencing the all-pervading space.

The Eighth Premise is:

The 'I' therefore, needs to be divested of the memories and the experiences, in the initial stages by reasoning out intellectually that these memories and the experiences are accretions to the gross body and not to the immaculate Self within. The phenomenal 'I' therefore do not constitute the real 'I'. The real 'I' or the Self is not aware of the body in deep sleep (*sushupti*) or even in sleep (*svapna*). In dreamless sleep (*sushupti*) the 'I' enjoys its own blissful BEING.

It is possible and, therefore, should be the endeavor of every one to be in that blissful state of awareness or of BEING, after realising that 'I' am not the body, not the memories nor the thoughts which go to make up the mind. 'I' am the Self, the blissful state which is enjoyed when the connection between the body and the memories is cut asunder.

The Ninth Premise is:

The way to disassociate the Self with the body and the memories is to ask, every time a thought comes, the query: 'To whom this thought arises ?' In other words, search the source of the thoughts, which collectively go to make up the phenomenal 'I'. As we enquire the source of the thought, the very thoughts will vanish and the mind will be free from the impressions created thereon.

The Tenth Premise is:

This is not easy and must be constantly adhered to by practice during the entire waking state. It is the nature of the mind to shift from one thought to the other. It is therefore necessary to restrain the mind and concentrate on a single thought as it arises and exclude all other thoughts creeping and interfering in the mind.

There are many methods for making the mind one pointed. But there is no one method which can be prescribed, suitable for all. Each one should adopt that method which is suitable for his temperament and according to his eligibility.

Control over the process of enquiry and restraining the mind becomes easier if the modifications which take place in mind are avoided or atleast slowed down. Restraint of breath, repetition of Mantras, company of the saints, visits to the temples and pilgrimage centres assist the process towards restraining the activity of the mind, in the first instance, and the destruction of the thoughts in the final stage. Then the Mind, shorn of the influences of the senses and impressions created thereupon, becomes a powerful instrument, pure in itself, capable of reflecting the Self which is within the core of the Heart.

Conclusion

Enquiring in to the nature of one's Self, the Self is released from the bondage of the thoughts, the memories, the experiences which go to make the ego, the conventional 'I', and makes the Self realise its true Blissful nature.

The above Premises are not exclusive nor are they exhaustive. For some they be guide, for others they may be confusing. They may help some; others have to fend for themselves and furrow their own path to walk, according to the stage of their spiritual development. In whichever circumstances, they will surely stimulate the intellect and clarify the mind. Of this they can be no doubt.